vine and honey

ben mark

100 Best Vines of All Time

Copyright

ISBN-13: 978-1-948191-05-0

ISBN-10: 1-948191-05-9

First Edition

Printed in the U.S.A

We dedicate this Book to All the Vine Creators and lovers

Table of Contents

Introduction

*"Vine was a way to see the world in a different light —
like re-imagining Drake's "Hotline Bling" as a tennis
match.*

It was a place to express your dreams.
It was also a place to share your needs.
And divulge your fears.
*Vine was a way to keep it real, even if confrontation
was necessary (with an expletive.)*

*Or just acknowledge that things might not be going
your way.*
It was a place to make a political statement.
*Because, after all, there was never any shame in
"doing it for the Vine"*
It was a place to show off your talents.
*Vine was a place to let loose, especially if you were a
duck with something to say.*

Or a cat with a penchant for Jason DeRulo.
*Or a dog who just wanted to dance to the dulcet tones
of Phil Collins.*

Vine provided an outlet to talk to your favorite athletes.
And to re-live your favorite sports moments.
Sometimes Vine was a platform for great art.
To share excellent covers of your favorite artist.
Or capturing unforgettable moments that you could play on loop."

We'll miss you, Vine!

100 Best Vines of all Times

you look exactly like mom

oh pls

don't insult me.

take one more picture

with my Dad

fuck that I aint

your fucking Dad

#celfies

hey carly

bye sweerie

B.I.T.C.H

guess what i just found out

your girl cheated on you with Mark

no

i got into Harvard...

Skrrrrrr

hello

yes it's Shushi

Heyyyy

well

i like my Women

how i like my coffee

Big tits

ooh yeah

this is ready to be plucked

ooh

soft n jucy

when the auxillary cable
is passed to you

im the captain Now

hey sup bae

when your bae is fam

hey

im sorry

i can't see there

austrism... mmmm

blocking all the haters

donut time

donut time

time to eat donut

what

murder time

murder time

time to murder who ate my donut

story time

in every group of friends

there is the dumb one

really?!?!

we in this bitch

finna get crunk

eyebrows on freek

da fuq

#onfleek

whats that

TRASH

Im dying

OMG

i gat one question for you

what are Those

ya'll gon make me

loose my mind

up in here

up in here

i don't get no fucking love from ya'll

ya'll gon get no love from me

when she says

she got a cute friend For You

OMG

why the fuck you lying
why you always lying

hollup hollup

gerarahere mehn

for a Moment

like this

im breaking up

with U

Screams... April Fool

im pregnant

Par

party is over

i gat it

here is the party

whats

the meaning of life

smoke weed and get em pictures

Im rick harrison

and this

Is my pawn shop

give me a boys name

that starts with the letter H

Hoe-ziah

hey

i got a surprise for you...

is that a chicken

nope...

didn't think so

tell me a part
of the body that
begins with the letter T

Tities

Ma niggah

two bruuhs

chilling in the hot tub

five feet apart

cause they're not gay

miss Kiesha

miss Kiesha

ooh my fuckin gawd

she fuckin dead

this bitch empty

yeet

hey where you goin

why you need to know
all up in my pussy boii

wtf if up kyle

no

what did you say

wtf dude

step the fuck up kyle

hi

welcome to chili's

im in me mom's car
vroom vroom

get out me car

awwwww

yeah! five inches deep in your moom!

to make a long story
short
i put a whole bag of jelly beans
up my ass

shower time
adderall
a glass of whiskey

and diesel jeans

i wanna be a cowboy

halloween is over

now

its chrismah

happy christums

merry chrisis

merry Chrysler

I'm getting myself a roll,

not a toilet paper roll

vine and honey

Zap, Zap

Losing me just by a fang bite

have any experience

with children
yeah

i chill all the time

can I borrow your hoe
sure

which one of em

shower time

adderall

a glass of whiskey

and diesel jeans

fuck everyone who's blind.

the only reason I'm doing this

is cos they'd never see it.

happy Birthday Grandpa

everyone I loved is gone

im still here Grandpa

everyone I loved is gone

why did the chicken cross the road

to get to the little bitches house

knock knock

who's there

the little chicken

wanna come play pool

on Saturday

nah

i can't swim

nice car

thanks

we should do dinner

what the fuck

wait! I never said it was my car

i forgive him

everyone gets cheated on

banging in the car boot

nope

i haven't seen him

I just had it

where is it

did you touch it

I swear to god

oh here it is.

I'd like chicken

with a side of sweater

hold the boyfriend

you're under arrest

but my belt was stuck

good night switty go to bed

why

because you need your rest

why

to grow big and strong baby

why

Smothers her with the pillow

two chocolate cones please

our machine is down

sighs

make that one chocolate cone

wake up! wake up!!
i got to ask you something

yawns

what

are you sleeping

7am
wakes up, picks up phone

7:15am
gets in to shower, drops phone on sink. Phone beeps. Rushes back to pick it up

7:25 am
wrapped in a towel, still on phone

8:39 am
running down the stairs, spilling coffee

damn... don't know why I'm always so fucking late

I goof with couz

Why

Umm

just cos

my dog died

that's too bad

you know my mom died too

why would you wanna make me more sad

is samantha here

raises hand

you don't look like a Samantha

shit happens

can I go to the bathroom
i don't know

can you

W.T.F

if Tomboys are real

then chickens can beatbox

whats your Name

diana

'Bitch you ain't diana

you diarrhea'

I just can't

say "hi"

to your cat for me

Wut?

i don't have a cat?

Its Your Damn Pussy Bitch

they left you alone to play

with yourself

that's why you always have

sticky arms

i came

i saw
and I was fuckin bored

when she's right

she's right
and when she's wrong

she's right

the party was mad

the party was lit

the party was

legitness

crickets

dont care how old she is
ass whooping is pretty blind

dead or alive
you aint hearing the end of this

pants down

ass whoop
it's a package deal

he's my nigga
shit or no shit

she's 18 bro
now I can fuck her past midnight

thank god for chickens

you're too old to be young man

my name's Savage
and I'm about to love you down

no one notices your ass when you're single

how's it going

not good

why

i found out i have A.D.D look

this says AIDS

thank god, I thought I had A.D.D

why you spend time with family so much
cos I fucking can

easy there love

i only like the jeans

dad

how did you meet mom

we was in school and we bumped into each other

her books fell

aww

and I see that ass I was like damn bitch

i think my heart's talking

no bro, you've just got gas

don't take away my mirror

it's where my best friend lives

what made you leave max at home

he said we'd netflix and chill

hey man

what happened to you

i called a black man

my niggah

what's so important

that you'd miss the game

my wife's pregnant

so?

y'all didn't have to fuck during the playoffs

how do I look

like a dumb fuck

i like your friends

why

they make me forget

I've got a *pig* at home

hey

treat him nice he's a human being

i know right

fucking hard to believe

hands in the air

what?

i thought I was your homie
justice is blind bitch

you're such a bore

you married whore

can i have a bite

Sur- fuck you dude

how i eat vs. instagrammers

me: *picks up pizza and put it in my mouth*

instagrammers: picks up phone click click click click thanks

we done

fuck my maths teacher

for making me believe

the answer to every question was X

can we go out to play

did you clean your room

like i asked you

did you cut the grass

like mom asked you

lawn mower churning

yeah

but that back flip thou

will your mouth

still remember the taste of

this *NUT*

i was wondering if

you could play that song again

which one mehn

the one that goes

hurt me... fuck me!

whoever

threw that paper

your mum's a

hoe

Thank You

Thank you for taking your time to Read our Tribute to the late and Great Vine (R.I.P). We wish to use this medium to thank all the Viners who Created this wonderful Content for us to watch and laugh our f*cking ass out, (*try not to Laugh or grin*).

And the Creators of Vine for Providing us with this Platform of expression.

Acknowledgement

Our Appreciation goes to

Kayla Newman

king bach

nick colletti,

Michael LoPriore

Curtis Lepore

Jordan Burt

Nash Grier

Brittany Furlan

Rudy Mancuso

Jessi Smiles

Logan Paul

Simone Shepherd

Manon Mathews... etc

Thanks for Creating these Masterpiece that spread through this amazing platform. Although, we'll miss vine. This Book, Vine and honey is truly a delight for the sensations, bringing back the riveting quotes we all laughed at together as a united internet community. Keep the fire of true comedy ablaze in your home By Getting a Copy of This Book.

Thanks So Much For The Support. If you Enjoyed Vine and honey

Take a Little Time to Leave Us A Review. It will be very much appreciated!

One or Two Statement Will Go a Long Way in Helping Other People Looking to Buy.

Follow Us on Facebook Here>>

https://www.facebook.com/vineandhoney/

Instagram Here:

Instagram @vineandhoney

Send Us Feedback Via >>
info@vineandhoney.com

CPSIA information can be obtained
at www.ICGtesting.com
Printed in the USA
LVHW02s2128231217
560697LV00034B/1761/P